Serbo-Croat/Bosnian and English Words for School Use

Riječi na srpsko-hrvatskom/bosanskom i engleskom jeziku za školsku upotrebu

London Borough
of Enfield
Arts And Libraries

Fj 3/04
DUAl SERBO-CROAT/
BOSNIAN + ENGLISH

30126 01732366 5

How to Use This Book

This book is one of a series of illustrated classroom word lists in languages spoken by refugee children. It is targeted at children who are newly-arrived in the UK and are beginning to learn English. It can also be used with children who have little or no literacy in Serbian, Croatian and Bosnian to help them develop reading and writing skills in these languages. A workbook for pupils accompanies this publication.

The classroom words can be used in different ways, for example

◆ to label pictures and classroom objects

◆ to match pictures to names. By using correcting fluid, you can erase English or Serbo-Croat/Bosnian words or pictures. Sets of cards can be made without names or illustrations, which can then be matched by the pupil

◆ to make games such as pelmanism, word bingo and snap

◆ to help pupils construct simple sentences

◆ to take home to copy, read and learn words, as an early homework task. All children who are beginning to learn English should be given homework if their classmates receive it, even though it needs to be very simple. Parents and carers can be encouraged to help their children with such tasks

◆ to help students develop literacy in Serbian/Croatian/Bosnian.

Serbo-Croat and English Words for School Use
Translated by Accent on type
Additional material compiled by Jill Rutter and Dina Mehmedbegovic
Photograph of Bosnian refugee child, his mother and grandmother, Tim Fox.
Designed by Artloud
Printed by Typecast
Copyright Refugee Council, 2001

While it is accepted that teachers may wish to copy this publication for educational purposes, no part of it may be reproduced for commercial purposes without prior written permission of the copyright owner. Applications for the copyright owner's permission should be addressed to the Refugee Council.

the refugee council

Registered as the British Refugee Council under the Charities Act 1960 No 1014576
Registered Company No 2727514
Registered Address 3 Bondway London SW8 1SJ

classroom **učionica, razred**

dining room **trpezarija/ blagovaonica**

library **biblioteka/knjižnica**

office **kancelarija/ured**

cloakroom **garderoba/ svlačionica**

playground **igralište**

teacher **učitelj, učiteljica; nastavnik, nastavnica**

book **knjiga**

bookcase **polica za knjige**

exercise book **sveska/teka**

blackboard **školska tabla / školska ploča**

computer **kompjuter / kompjutor, računalo**

toys **igračke**

ball **lopta**

pen **pero, hemijska olovka /
k**emijska olovka****

pencil **olovka**

scissors **makaze/škare**

ruler **lenjir/ravnalo**

rubber **guma za brisanje**

school bag **školska tašna /
školska torba**

paintbrush **četka/kist**

chair **stolica**

table **sto/stol**

clock **časovnik/sat**

People **Ljudi**

man **čovek/čovjek**

woman **žena**

children **deca/djeca**

boy **dečak/dječak**

girl **devojka/djevojka**

baby **beba**

doctor **doktor, lekar / liječnik**

nurse **medicinska sestra**

farmer **poljoprivrednik**

secretary **sekretar, sekretarica / tajnik, tajnica**

shop assistant **prodavač, prodavačica**

carpenter **stolar**

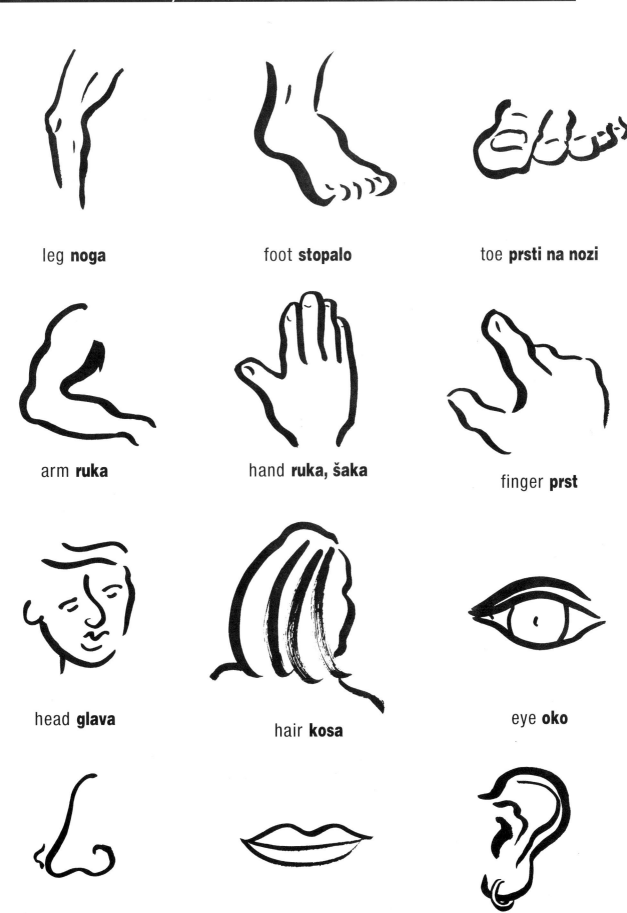

leg **noga**

foot **stopalo**

toe **prsti na nozi**

arm **ruka**

hand **ruka, šaka**

finger **prst**

head **glava**

hair **kosa**

eye **oko**

nose **nos**

mouth **usta**

ear **uho**

Clothes **Odeća/Odjeća**

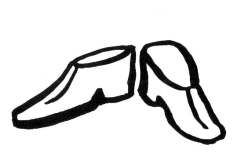

shoes **cipele**

trainers **patike/tenisice**

sandals **sandale**

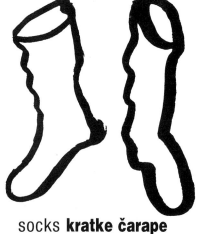

socks **kratke čarape**

coat **kaput**

hat **kapa, šešir**

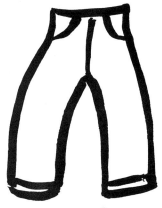

trousers **pantalone/hlače**

shirt **košulja**

jumper, pullover
džemper, pulover

skirt **suknja**

dress **haljina**

tie **mašna/kravata**

knickers, pants
gaćice, donje gaće

vest **potkošulja**

cardigan **džemper na zakopčavanje**

shorts **šorc / kratke hlače**

tee-shirt **majica s kratkim rukavima**

tights **jednodelne čarape / hulahupke**

watch **ručni časovnik / ručni sat**

gloves
rukavice

raincoat
kišni mantil

scarf **marama, šal**

bag **tašna/torba**

umbrella **kišobran**

9

Animals **Životinje**

cow **krava**

calf **tele**

sheep **ovca**

lamb **jagnje/janje**

goat **koza**

pig **svinja**

cat **mačka**

kitten **mače, mačić**

dog **pas**

puppy **štene, kuče /
psetance, psić**

mouse **miš**

rabbit **zec**

fox **lisica**

bird **ptica**

elephant **slon**

lion **lav**

monkey **majmun**

bear **medved/medvjed**

fly **muva/muha**

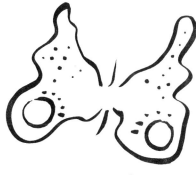

butterfly **leptir**

snake **zmija**

worm **crv**

frog **žaba**

bee **pčela**

11

camel **kamila/deva**

horse **konj**

tractor **traktor**

lorry **kamion**

boat **čamac**

bicycle **bicikl**

train **voz/vlak**

bus **autobus**

car **auto, automobil**

donkey **magarac**

pushchair **dečija kolica /
dječja kolica**

aeroplane **avion/zrakoplov**

Fruit and Vegetables **Voće i povrće**

potato **krompir/krumpir**

onion **luk**

tomato **paradajz/rajčica**

carrot **šargarepa/mrkva**

cauliflower **karfiol/cvjetača**

lettuce **zelena salata**

cucumber **krastavac**

spinach **spanać/špinat**

orange **pomorandža/naranča**

apple **jabuka**

banana **banana**

lemon **limun**

Food **Hrana**

bread **hleb / hljeb, kruh**

fish **riba**

eggs **jaja**

chicken **pile**

meat **meso**

cheese **sir**

sugar **šećer**

flour **brašno**

rice **pirinač/riža**

salt **so/sol**

soup **supa/juha**

spagetti **špageti**

salad **salata**

chips **pomfrit**

tea **čaj**

coffee **kafa/kava**

milk **mleko/mlijeko**

water **voda**

biscuits **keksi**

cake **kolač, torta**

sandwich **sendvič**

sweets **bombone/bomboni**

lentils **sočivo / sočivica, leća**

tinned food
**hrana u konzervi,
hrana u limenki**

15

The Kitchen **Kuhinja**

cooker **šporet/štednjak**

fridge **frižider/hladnjak**

washing machine **vešmašina /
stroj za pranje rublja**

sink **slivnik, sudoper**

cupboard **orman s policama /
ormar s policama**

pot, saucepan **šerpa, lonac /
zdjela**
pan **tiganj, tava**

knife **nož**

fork **viljuška**

spoon **kašika/žlica**

plate **tanjir/tanjur**

cup **šolja/šalica**

glass **čaša**

The Bathroom **Kupatilo/Kupaona**

toilet **toalet, WC**

bath **kada**

shower **tuš**

washbasin **lavabo/umivaonik**

toothbrush **četkica za zube**

toothpaste **pasta za zube**

teeth **zubi**

towel **peškir/ručnik**

comb **češalj**

soap **sapun**

shampoo **šampon**

tap
slavina/pipa

17

My House and My Garden Moja kuća i bašta / Moja kuća i vrt

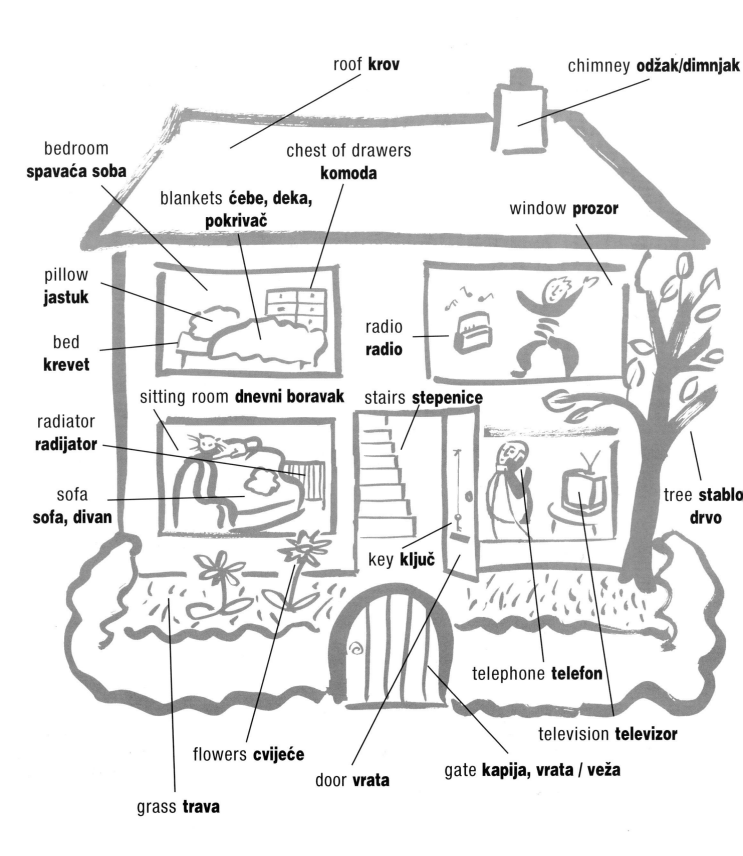

roof **krov**

chimney **odžak/dimnjak**

bedroom **spavaća soba**

chest of drawers **komoda**

blankets **ćebe, deka, pokrivač**

window **prozor**

pillow **jastuk**

radio **radio**

bed **krevet**

sitting room **dnevni boravak**

stairs **stepenice**

radiator **radijator**

tree **stablo drvo**

sofa **sofa, divan**

key **ključ**

telephone **telefon**

flowers **cvijeće**

door **vrata**

gate **kapija, vrata / veža**

television **televizor**

grass **trava**

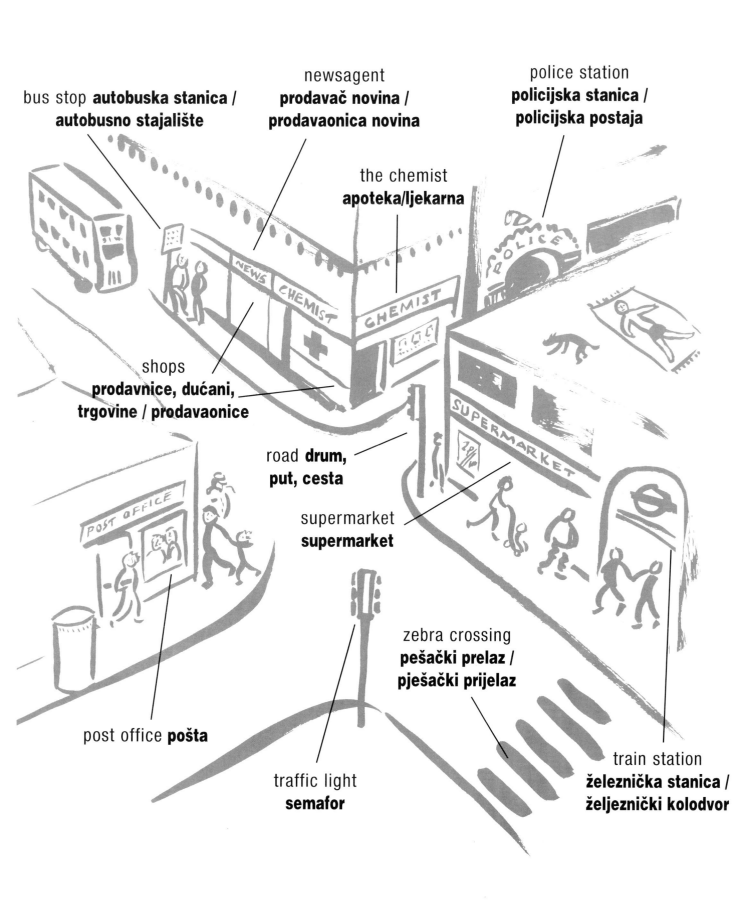

newsagent
**prodavač novina /
prodavaonica novina**

police station
**policijska stanica /
policijska postaja**

bus stop **autobuska stanica /
autobusno stajalište**

the chemist
apoteka/ljekarna

shops
**prodavnice, dućani,
trgovine / prodavaonice**

road **drum,
put, cesta**

supermarket
supermarket

post office **pošta**

zebra crossing
**pešački prelaz /
pješački prijelaz**

train station
**željeznička stanica /
željeznički kolodvor**

traffic light
semafor

19

Numbers **Brojevi**

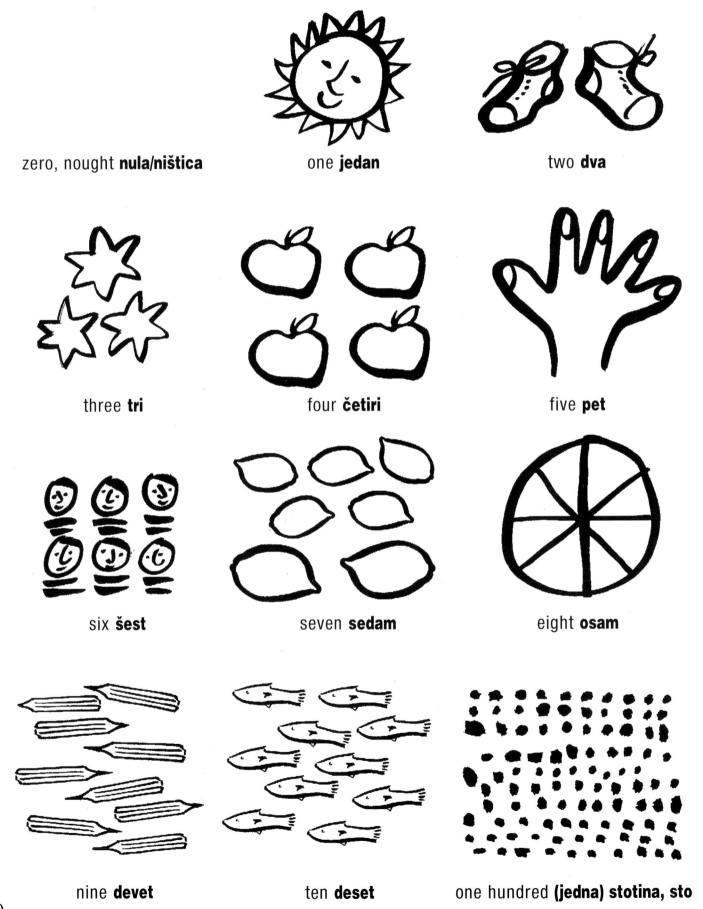

zero, nought **nula/ništica**

one **jedan**

two **dva**

three **tri**

four **četiri**

five **pet**

six **šest**

seven **sedam**

eight **osam**

nine **devet**

ten **deset**

one hundred **(jedna) stotina, sto**

Words and Phrases Riječi i fraze

Numbers Brojevi

eleven **jedanaest**
twelve **dvanaest**
thirteen **trinaest**
fourteen **četrnaest**
fifteen **petnaest**
sixteen **šesnaest**
seventeen **sedamnaest**
eighteen **osamnaest**
nineteen **devatnaest**
twenty **dvadeset**
twenty one **dvadeset jedan**
thirty **trideset**
forty **četrdeset**
fifty **pedeset**
sixty **šezdeset**
seventy **sedamdeset**
eighty **osamdeset**
ninety **devedeset**
one hundred **jedna stotina, sto**
one thousand **(jedna) hiljada / (jedna) tisuća**

yes **da**
no **ne**
please **molim**
thankyou **hvala**

hello **zdravo**
goodbye **doviđenja**

My name is **Ime mi je, Zovem se**
My address is **Moja adresa je**
My telephone number is **Moj broj telefona je**
My teacher's name is **Moj(a) učitelj(ica) se zove**

cold **hladno**
hot **toplo, vruće**
I feel ill **Loše se osećam / Loše se osjećam**
I have stomach ache **Boli me stomak / Boli me želudac**
I have a cold **Imam nazeb, prehlađen(a) sam**
I have a headache **Boli me glava**

Lessons Nastava

maths **matematika**
English **engleski**
science **prirodne nauke (biologija, fizika, hemija/kemija)**
history **historija/povijest**
geography **geografija/zemljopis**
French **francuski**
art **likovna umetnost / likovna umjetnost**
music **muzičko vaspitanje / muzički odgoj**
PE/games **fiskultura / timske igre**

Meals Obroci/Objedi

breakfast **doručak**
lunch (snack) **ručak, užina**
supper, dinner **večera**

left **levo/lijevo**
right **desno**

morning **jutro**
noon **podne**
afternoon **popodne**
evening **veče/večer**
night **noć**

Days of the week Dani u sedmici / Dani u tjednu

Monday **ponedeljak/ ponedjeljak**
Tuesday **utorak**
Wednesday **sreda/srijeda**
Thursday **četvrtak**
Friday **petak**
Saturday **subota**
Sunday **nedelja/nedjelja**

Months of the year Meseci u godini / Mjeseci u godini

January **januar/siječanj**
February **februar/veljača**
March **mart/ožujak**
April **april/travanj**
May **maj/svibanj**
June **juni/lipanj**
July **juli/srpanj**
August **august/kolovoz**
September **septembar/rujan**
October **oktobar/listopad**
November **novembar/studeni**
December **decembar/prosinac**

The seasons Godišnja doba

spring **proleće/proljeće**
summer **leto/ljeto**
autumn **jesen**
winter **zima**

Weather Vreme/Vrijeme

rain **kiša**
sun **sunce**
wind **vetar/vjetar**
snow **sneg/snijeg**

Relatives Rođaci

parents **roditelji**
foster parents **staratelji**
father **otac**
mother **majka**
son **sin**
daughter **kćerka, kći**
grandfather **deda/djed**
grandmother **baka**
uncle **stric**
aunt **tetka/teta**
cousin (first) **brat (sestra) od strica, brat (sestra) od tetke; bratić (bratična), sestrić (sestrična)**

21

AUSTRIA

HUNGARY

■ Maribor

SLOVENIA

■ Subotica

ROMANIA

■ Zagreb

Ljubjana

CROATIA

Osijek ■

■ Novi Sad

■ Rijeka

Belgrade ■

Banja Luka ■

BOSNIA

HERZEGOVINA

■ Kragujevac

Sarajevo ■

SERBIA

Split

■

Prishtina

Sofia

■

MONTENEGRO

■

KOSOVA

Podgorica

■

BULGARIA

Shkoder

■

Skopje

■

Tetovo

Strumica

ADRIATIC SEA

MACEDONIA

■

ITALY

■ Tirana

■ Ohrid

Salonica

■

ALBANIA

GREECE

MEDITERRANEAN SEA

22

Serbian, Croatian and Bosnian Speaking Refugees

Refugees have been fleeing former Yugoslavia since 1991. The first refugees were mostly Croats displaced by fighting in 1991. Many of them returned home after the UN-brokered ceasefire. The next group who arrived in the UK were Bosnians, fleeing fighting which lasted from 1992–1995. The Bosnians came in three waves:

- those who arrived by themselves and have applied for political asylum

- those who were who brought to the UK by voluntary organisations on convoys. Most of them applied for political asylum

- former prison camp detainees, plus medical evacuees who have been admitted as part of a British Government programme administered by the Refugee Council and other charities between 1992 and 1995.

Almost all the Bosnians spoke Serbo-Croat (or Bosnian as they preferred to describe it) as their first language. Since then, other Serbo-Croat speaking refugees have fled to the UK, including Croatian Serbs, people from mixed marriages, Serbian peace activists and political opposition, a small number of men who did not wish to serve in the Yugoslav People's Army during the Bosnian or Kosovan conflict, Roma from Serbia, Croatia and Kosovo.

Serbo-Croat, Slovenian and Macedonian were the official languages of former Yugoslavia,

with Serbo-Croat being the language of government. Serbo-Croat, Slovenian and Macedonian are southern Slavonic languages.

Until 1992 Serbo-Croat was generally considered as one language. It was spoken in much of Croatia, Serbia, Bosnia and Montenegro. Since the collapse of former Yugoslavia, it is now customary to call Serbo-Croat either Serbian, Croatian or Bosnian, although the 'new' languages are very similar. Some Montenegrin nationalists also claim that there is a separate 'Montenegrin' language. However, Serbian, Croatian and Bosnian show differences in spelling and vocabulary. As time goes by, greater differences will emerge.

It is easy to identify a Serbian, Croatian or Bosnian person's origin by their accent, dialect and use of words. Most 'Serbo-Croat' dialects are mutually intelligible. Serbs and Croats may use different words for particular things, for example Serbs will use the word *igra* for dance, while Croatian uses *ples*. Serbian has tended to borrow international terms from other languages, while Croatian uses its own words – for example *biblioteka* (Serbian for library) and *knjižica* (Croatian).

Serbian, as spoken in Serbia and Montenegro, is usually written in the Cyrillic script (known there as *Azbuka*). Bosnian and Croatian are written using the Roman alphabet.

The Serbo-Croat Alphabet

Roman		Cyrillic	
a	A	а	А
b	B	б	Б
c	C	в	В
č	Č	г	Г
ć	Ć	д	А
d	D	ђ	Ђ
đ	Đ (dj Dj)	е	Е
dž	Dž	ж	Ж
e	E	з	З
f	F	и	И
g	G	ј	Ј
h	H	к	К
i	I	л	Л
j	J	љ	Љ
k	K	м	М
l	L	н	Н
lj	Lj	њ	Њ
m	m	о	О
n	n	п	П
nj	Nj	р	Р
o	O	с	С
p	P	т	Т
r	R	ħ	Ђ
s	S	у	У
š	Š	ф	Ф
t	T	х	Х
u	U	ц	Ц
v	V	ч	Ч
z	Z	џ	Џ
ž	Ž	ш	Ш